THE BURNING EAVES

Also by David Manicom

Poetry

Sense of Season (Press Porcépic, 1989)
Theology of Swallows (Oolichan Books, 1991)
The Older Graces (Oolichan Books, 1997)

Fiction

Ice in Dark Water (Véhicule, 1997)

Non-fiction:

Progeny of Ghosts (Oolichan Books, 1998)

The Burning Eaves

POEMS BY

David Manicom

OOLICHAN BOOKS
LANTZVILLE, BRITISH COLUMBIA, CANADA
2003

National Library of Canada Cataloguing in Publication Data

Manicom, David, 1960-
The burning eaves / David Manicom.

Poems.
ISBN 0-88982-224-7

I. Title.
PS8576.A545B87 2003   C811'.54   C2003-910630-6
PR9199.3.M3485B87 2003

Le Conseil des Arts | The Canada Council
du Canada | for the Arts

We gratefully acknowledge the support of the Canada Council for the Arts for our publishing program.

BRITISH
COLUMBIA
ARTS COUNCIL
Supported by the Province of British Columbia

Grateful acknowledgement is also made to the BC Ministry of Tourism, Small Business and Culture for their financial support.

Canadä

We acknowledge the financial support of the Government of Canada through the Book Publishing Industry Development Program for our publishing activities.

Published by
Oolichan Books
P.O. Box 10, Lantzville
British Columbia, Canada
V0R 2H0

Printed in Canada

For Adrian, Mr. A, and for Momma Jean

Acknowledgements

Some poems first appeared, often in different versions, in the magazines *Matrix*, *Malahat Review*, and *Fiddlehead*. My thanks to the editors for their support. A special thanks to first readers Charles Foran and Teresa Marquis, and to Ross Leckie at *Fiddlehead* for giving so many of these a first airing. My debt to Ron Smith at Oolichan remains unpayable.

"Nothing is too wonderful to be true."
—Michael Faraday

" . . . there's nothing uglier than a man
hitting his stride."
—The Tragically Hip

Contents

Year of Storm

Tal

Under the Champlain Sea

The Late Qing

The Shadow Photon

Coda

1

Year of Storm

Reading Anglo-Saxon When Spring Comes Early

Aquiver after the downward plunge, firelit silver—
A dagger in a table top, rude trestle, mead—

The feasters sheered into vision from their venison
And victory songs by the sight of one slight sparrow

Passing from snowing darkness through their narrow hall
And into the night again. A life.

One winter evening, pinioned on the bus from work,
I wrote: *So arrival of each hoped-for future*

Means a hoped-for future lost—

Closing the phrase behind me as an awkward wing,
The lurching muteness, the bus like the apostrophe

Before possession, that still walk home.
The Outaouais
                    turns its slow, northern curve around the town

Into a dipping gallop through the gull-thick narrows
At Deschênes, and away, its speed below the yards

—Its silver plunge and sinuosity—clearing
The gaze for elevation, away in every aspect

From the gravelly streets and the plump knuckling
Of the branches when spring comes before its time

With the cardinals' big whistle out of old realms of cedar
Through each warmer dawn, and a row of daffodils

All facing one way beneath our windowsill
With ruched collar-frills, as yellow as if our youngest child

Had filled them in with crayon. To lift the angle
Of the wing. Up the street where a chorale of tulips

Surrounds a garden's centrepiece of stone
I find my Flora and Antaeus selves, can't stop

Forever living in more than one myth, with doubling
Arrivals into loss. . . . Whereas the tulips

Delayed by the special beauty of delay (to lift)
Are not quite open until, at least, tomorrow—

Grooved, upheld, waxy, pursed: two prayerful hands,
So that along the swelling pods a blush of red, of white:

The seam
Of the cardinal, the sparrow, of the long, long horizon.

When May is Also a Month of Mourning

The mantle awake, we swam early this year
In the weather-shadow of dream volcanoes.

When the thought arises, what else goes under?
What flounders then, awash, as twilight seals the surfaces?

Like a death in May, like a toddler still awake
To the undercoat our language slurs away

("What colour are your eyes?" *They blue and black and white. . . .*),

Or lilac blossoms on a field of green: this week
Plain garden borders and parkland filler have obeyed

Deep longings of our season they in turn compose—
Or what of the frozen patterns of the stars?

Ice chips of fire for the iron furnace
Burning behind the thrumming glassy blue—Firm sky

Behind high cirrus tufts combed thin where upper winds
Sweep back the promenades of cumulus

Beyond our wincing lids, the watery lens of air . . . .
What depends on all this layering of veils?

—·—

Patterns in turn bud silently as lesions
From the opaque surface tension of all evenings

Into these pendulous armfuls of blossoms,
                              these ambushes of scent—

Both here where I awaited sheer damned beauty
And everywhere I failed to see what to expect.

I admit the feedback loop of a natural reading,
A reading into things—But there is more, besides,

The ablation, the eye-glow of burning mountaintops,
More besides the undercoat of white

Where the receding Outaouais contracts a gaze
Of close-to-the-water angles on the first day in,

Its high spring wash
              Like a slung whip along riverbanks overhung
With the soft burst cones of mauve perfume

Slowing the walk homeward from the white, flaked skull
Tenderly brittle and bare, in wisps of down—

A mother's drawstring mouth pulling at milky dark
As her raking talon twists the curtain back

A thrombus of every inclination

Until no words or what they rise from can be settled to—
Presence, overwhelm, lonely, true, devote,

Even *dignity* too grandiloquent a word,
Word a word,

Folding down and in, not to speak of the sound
Of the breathing. Lilac flowers from the green bush,

At each stroke I swim forward pushing off
Something else pushing back.

July Dusk Singularity

*"Because space itself, not only matter, was all contained
within the pinpoint that preceded the Big Bang, the correct
answer to the question 'Where did it take place?' is 'here.'*
—Timothy Ferris

Though it felt like your touch at last, under my eye,
High on the cheekbone's zone of sun and rain,

Walking—watching night's mask lowering as if it came
To settle in the end on a face of painted wood,

Where after the hottest hours the feathery splendour
Of Black Walnut harbours a gulf of purer void,

Inhaled stillness held against the oyster sky's
Patient preparation for sudden flight.

The bats fold, fold, outflung hands above the lawns,
Each of my words, meanings of you, creased and turned

On its own opening, like the day, like the days.
The dark mass of fallen walnuts press the earth

In deepening grass, bearings of olive leather.

Watching—walking far enough from home
To speak to you aloud, roaming toward

The enclosure of a beginning so closely sewn
Into our fabric's seamlessness that the explosion

Took place with everywhere ending here, on and on
Through the leather weight in the shadowed dusk.

Losing you, the mesh aligns; the fineness of the pain
Remains the line between my face without you, and the dark,

First whisper out of silence lifting the static fields
Breathed in to meet the last small sound, and sealed.

In spite of appearances, drawing you everywhere,
There was, in the beginning, nowhere but here.

September Gale with High Theory

Windy all day and now through a restless night
The gusts bodychecking the century timbers.

Early leavetaking of leaves in the year of storm,
All summer expected highs surpassed, the norms belied--

Though forecasters continue to rely on their weather
Systems, a scholasticism of thunder and sun,

While the telescopes study at a great remove
The history of the periodic table.

September still. Yet curled leaves the colour of old maps
Already fill each gap of hedge, heap under cedars

Or catch, tattering in chain-link.
But no season so unseasonal as to make us shrink

From the laws of nature, from the nature of having laws—
The physicists unwrap flaw after flaw, yet all fall

I've read in vain for the claim there are no laws at all.
Amid coat-rack trees after a day of gales

A singular maple is still crayola crimson
In the abandoned lot across the corner,

Flaring above a brake of lilac's barren ribs.
Hung in the pure air between

A squirrel pauses like a kink in the telephone line,
The wind whines through the wires, reaps the trees,

Two oak leaves settle on the porch like copper gloves.
All circles prove ellipses, the long slopes of gravity

Disappear into each singularity
(That empty shell without a shell),

Into the purer art of gauge bosons and charms;
An alarm of red-shifts, new measurements required—

And the hesitancy of the particles
That never exist in one particular place

Is my longing to unlace this thought without motion.
In the end, the beginning, the great inflation

Everywhere found in the wind of the same place—
Before the bang, in theory, mere fold of empty space

Not even hovering, not even silent, not even
"the field dancing out of the braking cosmic vacuum."

A November storm rocks our old house in September,
Creaks the walls like bedsprings under love.

Awake in the meantime, ears strained, a single word
Speaks flat and disembodied down the hall—

Leaf of small moan from my child dreaming,
The seam of a seam, a palm that opens and turns.

The Slowing of Light

The declension of light pulls down the crown of trees—
More intimate hands now, more intimate destinies

In the narrow aperture of November afternoons,
Where town squares dim to the faint luminescence

Of their cenotaphs, loom of granite in a grey lake.
Dark before five, decanting a sense of lives that brake hard

Into this sort of air. Some I am spared, some I live.
For now I believe with the belief of desire

In our early walk home, ice in the pores of the asphalt
Like salt in the earth, a few pearls in the headlights

And the snowy rain caught as bright netting in your hair.
The instruments are delicate enough to now declare

The decay of orbits; then this week the papers
Report the faltering constant of the speed of light—

If the math is right all sight was swifter in the past,
In the asymptotic, soaring apse of space.

A hockey net abandoned to the early dark
Stands at our garage as the growing up of sons,

A stick flossed on slapshots leans against the porch,
Leans against the soaring apse of space.

We go in, we are going on together,
The light each day one finest hairbreadth slower

Until at the end of time your glance upward from the pillow
Will take forever to reach my waiting eyes.

2

Tal

"There are so many teasing words (in the Burushaski language), so many sweet words, so many mysterious words. For example, the word 'tal' can mean so many things: a kind of bird, the roof of your mouth, a grass in the fields, a birch tree, the ceiling of a room, motionless water."

— Allamah Nasir Hunzai

1. *A Kind of Bird*

My teasing word, *tal*, is a kind of bird,
The first bird seen by the recently blind,

Crossing the street-shade from tree to tree,
A heart-drop of parakeet green, the fade

Of its trail in the mind your fingers asleep
On my back as I ease from your veil,

Its tropical tail the feather in its cap,
Snake-flick after slinging of wings, as if to fail

At the art of flight—then a quick little lick
In the middle of things.

2. The Roof of the Mouth

Awake at dawn, an exiled emperor,
I hear the peacocks scream, have lost my tongue.

I wanted you close as the roof of my mouth.
Tal. With you through years I became a truth

Which, almost silent, we could only hear
When soft on hard the touch came twice,

First *T*, then *L*. The years. I found no device
Closer, for moving in, through where my eyes

Searching for your outerness began
To see the cast of their reflection.

3. *A Grass in the Field*

High on the terraced hillsides of Swat
We sat in the cloud lap while apricot

Blossomed like slow snow in the valleys
And spring undid the streambeds' silver laces.

We breathed the air of the great circle
Until, as I reached to furrow your hair,

My hand brushed the face of the Hindu Kush.
In that drunk hum of air a hollow lurched

As you laughed and arched and the wind wheeled.
"Touch me," you said, "a grass in the field."

4. *A Birch Tree*

By then the leaves were down, like an old paper sun
Torn at the height of the *fête*, drifts of pollen

Near the abandoned capital of summer,
Sussex cottages high in the green Gallies

Dreamed relentlessly by the brick-oven plains
Of Sindh, white even in the autumn rains,

White in woodshadow, white where the village girls
Crouched sickle-ing grass in the clearing below,

Clean bone of crescent moon, one finger-
Tip along a half-lit thigh: *tal*, birch, *soon*.

5. *The Ceiling of a Room*

Taxila's leggo outline; Qumran floorplan; a deeper
Palace of Troy. Firepit and wall-joint. Basement confine . . .

Or my lifelong excavation, my dig toward a root
That proved but layer on layer of sky. Had I known.

Or you, curved above me and pushing down
As if to fit a finger to your eternal ring.

My eyes dissolved the plaster dawn beyond your hair;
Afterward, we were footings, cobbled together.

But that upward gaze is safely ours. They fail to find
What they are digging through. *Listen.* Delicate spade.

Stop. Feather brush. *Resume.* They can never lay bare
The ceiling of a lovers' room.

6. *Motionless Water*

Inside, out, tip of your tongue on the roof
Of my mouth, the strange dark swimming, the glide

Of the dusk parakeet into this still frame
Where somehow all we are has been arranged,

Grasses poised and the pale curves of birch
Set beside the marbled surface of the pool,

Clouds floated into the reeds, the oil wash
Of evening water glazing the sky's hood, the ceiling

Fluttering ever so slightly overhead
Or underneath the dimming, held, elemental *tal.*

3

Under the Champlain Sea

The Burning Eaves

Fire to the level of my eyes, into the trees
Whose leaves now merge their colours with the birds;
Angle of sun beneath our porch's eaves
To catch at last this kitchen-window sink.

I pull white plates from grey beneath the foam
Like shells emerging from our portioned sea.
Rinsed, they shine. Brief in the rack, then swaddled
In the tea towel, in your hands. Scrub and dip and pass

As the louvered pattern of the shutters' shadow
Bands your wrists with their late summer source.
All grief is captured by the acts of love,
In how we work to hand things back and forth.

Under the Champlain Sea

Five hundred feet above the flags and houses
A burning skin encloses, heaves

At its pins, relieves the pressures of the moon.
Underside of a vast spoon. Cap of thinking.

You will have to sink, and swim, with me,
For I have seen the invisible seam that shows

How our pretty new home, in first November snow,
Rests deep below the vanished Champlain Sea.

A matter of history. A sewing box of centuries.
A later age. We live where ocean drained away.

So breathe in me. I'll breathe in you. We'll breathe devotion.
The sun goes over like a lover in a mirror.

Persistence

(Dew)

A white basin is refilled, dawn follows dawn.
Someone finds the children lunch, and tidies up. At one
The window blinds are drawn against an August sun.

Now every day alone, she must call each name
And tell them stories of the end of love.
The bedrooms on the second floor are dim;
Torpid leaves swim slowly on a pulsing screen.
Her hair, against her face, is dampened by the cloth
Whose coolness is renewed by unseen hands
That pass throughout the creak and shutter of the day.
The white basin is refilled with water.
The grandparents learn to tend a middle year.
They will lay the cloth of evening and dew
On her hot dry eyes, will wait with her
As one waits with the very old, though she is young.

She hears her children playing in the yards below;
But their words do not resolve, their voices intertwine
As if the codes have been forgotten, as if the cloth
Were balm against both family names and light.

(The Goldfinch)

A finch appears and disappears at the feeder perch—
Small lurchings of the world, feathers of the eye.
*Gold*finch: jet design against the yellow bib.
The empty plate, a white mirror, a sip of juice
Then mama gone to the distant sink, loosed from your fist
That bangs through your gaze on the chair's blank tray. Wistful
Dishes. Slow cloth circles the bright disk.

Laid on your back: wand of gravity, a flue of light.
Like your weather, the white vessel waits to reappear.
Your hand rises from the underworld
Into new fields where her feathery lashes shine
Like the birds sounding air with us, just out of view.

The planes depart, white yarn across the inlet blue.
The sun comes clear into the lawn, the long shadows
Persist again in their true, invisible furrows.

Separated

Beyond reach. Days of winter rain into graining snow.
Low drapes of mist as colour-drained as the silent rain
Passing through its hovering into each separate field
Along the concealed lanes, through drifting holds of mist
That reveals the rain lost within the movement of itself.

Dirt-and-water windowpane like a migraine lens.
A world of fens beyond the barns, the once firm ground.
A painter alarmed before a canvas growing fainter
In diluting winter, I went out in my father's boots,
A careful footing in the sluicing of the snow.

The ghost was below. The fields, just beneath the breath
And slow sift of rain, were stretched and dangerously thin,
Field the colour of corn husk forgotten in the bin,
Bandaged with snow, dimming again in unseasonal rain,
The winter day draining through the movement of itself.

Abstain. Sustain. Maintain. And later: replace, regain.
Near the corn crib's grey timbers and rusty webbing
Rain rapped its corrugated roof, house for weeds and crows.
The damping blows came through me, native to my captured calm:
Sustain. Maintain. The sentence of a winter farm.

From the hilltop turning-back the house could not emerge
From the photographic fluid of the rain, walls of fog
A slightly-lit montage, an all-suspending silver
Belying open plain of winter and an outer light,
Pressure, a brightening membrane, this continuance.

Fast

Eid-ul-Fitr, Ash Wednesday and Basant
Coincide this year, overlaid on my dormant faith,
On the wraiths I keep beyond. I lie furled
Where the mild February sun on Islamabad
Shows spring crevices in the tor and ziggurat pines
Along the cut-out spine of the Margalla hills.
At their profile, I'm sure, a local heartstring pulls.

My son is a dragon. It's Chinese New Year too.

———

Emblematically, perhaps, the jacarandas wait
For the purple canopies of March. Basant kites—
Litter raised to new heights—strain and flitter
Over all castes of roofs, strings suturing a tie-died sky.
Parakeets cry a colour and scythe themselves
Out of shadows, sweeps of green the fervour
Of someone's myth. It's long since the last big slaughter.
The Hindu shrines grow grass.

                              To end the Ramadan fast,
The long dry days, wooly feast-goats bleat on their leads
Beside dumpsters up and down the streets, dead
With the new moon, bled for the new moon.

———

Here I can assume only symbols, which lie
Much deeper in the eyes of Punjabis and Pathans.
Morning Mozart split by an off-key call to prayer,
I hear a riverbed of longing mourn
From the tin-horn speakers of the local mosque,
The sound of the desert yearning for more thirst,
Ashes begging more fire. But I curse *kazan*
Each weekday five a.m., craving mere sleep
To haul me through another week of work.
Tomorrow goat offal will rot in the dumpsters;
The feasters will sleep late; my love and I
Will wash off the cross of ash without a sigh.

We let fall our lenten sacrifice soon after lunch.
I find you just out of the tub, hunched to brush
Your lush hair willowing toward the floor, breasts bare,
A towel saronged without care around your waist
Like Gaugin's Western image of the East. Homage
Overdue, I first rummage for the toothpaste
But catch the ghosted voices of the VCR
Accounting for the kids, and slowly restore
The curve of your stooping back with fingertips
Fluting your spine, with lips and palms and arms—
Until you dash out of the warm mist
And duck back in with a condom, turn the lock.

———

The bray of the balloon-wallah's horn in the street,
Bell of the beggar with his shuffling bear
All day long on Eid-ul-Fitr, Ash Wednesday
And Basant, my eyes closed in your wet hair,
A shower curtain's foilage is my finest vista.
The heater whirs behind you in the steam
Making do as a hearth while we make leaning love
(A little tricky) up against the vanity.

The Convex Mirror

a translation of "Le Miroir courbé" by Yves Bonnefoy

1

Look at them, there at the crossroads,
Who seem to hesitate, who set out again.
The child runs before them: they have gathered
In great armfuls for the few vases
Those meadowland flowers which have no names.

And the angel who watches them is above,
Enveloped in the gale of his colours.
One arm is bare in the red stuff of air
As if he holds a mirror, as if the earth
Is reflected in the water of this other shore.

And what does he indicate now, with a finger
That points to one place in this image?
Is it another house, or another world,
Is it a very doorway in the light,
Light intermingled of things and signs?

2

They love to come back late like this. No longer
Can they perceive even the road among the stones
Where a red ochre shadow rises still.
Yet they have faith. Close to the threshold
The grass is supple and there is no death.

And now they are here beneath the arches.
It grows dark among the rumour of dry leaves
That are made to move upon the flagstones
By a wind that does not know, from room to room,
What have names, and what are simply things.

They go. They go. There among the ruins
Is the country where the banks are calm,
The paths unmoving. In the rooms
They will place the flowers close to the mirror
That might consume, that might preserve.

Recovery

This is
Sweetest
As lust
Desists,
Sweetest
Just as
Rushes
In breezes
Rise,
Just as
The tense
Remove
Goes back
Inside;
This is
Longest
In Shortest
Space, is
Easiest
As your slow
Lather, goes
Like the sky's
Long cry
Inward, sprung,
Flicked tongue

Renewed
On nipples'
New tips
And the still
Electric
Clit,
The bow
Undone
Sweetest
To the taste
With your
Slick ether's
Aftermath,
Bow sprung,
Slack
And undone,
Sweet
With the lack,
Tilting back
With the ache
And ache's lack
To come.

Prone

Have we turned away from all true openings
In holding to the closure of our love?
There were burnt lemon leaves on the ochre brick;

The garden culled them from the sky's collage;
Each one as it fell remade the form
Of what is seen from here, the toll of light.

They say so simply, "She flung herself down."
The question couldn't be figure to the garden;
Not all possible transformations lay within

The circle we had drawn. Torn chrysalis,
She begged "just be you." Let's not pretend
We never shape our settling down with fire.

Wakefield

Slow sunlight of honey in the jar.
Evening river; eyelids of the banks.
Into waterglass peace, like drops of ink,
Blues swell from the door of the waterfront bar.

Later, carlights fan across the village curve,
Flatline strobes into the park's deep calm.
Each showed me one half of your face. My nerve
Twitched. Your voice falters always, but goes on.

(When at last you arrive)

At the ends of the earth, gaunt, cormorants dive
Into the smoked lens of evening river;
In muted solitudes seize it—silver, live—
Throats collared with their owners' hunger.

She squats where the village path will always end
At the River Li, at the outcrop's lip.
At the ends of the earth the cloth is wrung out.
My eye dies slowly, scrollwork of the final drop.

Karst hills soared into the classic mist, my boat
Held on the orbit of her hands' tourniquet.
To filament of spring bamboo, as her wrists
Grip again and twist, a swallow settles, lists.

I saw her from the evening bus's wickerwork of light:
Last customer in Starbucks, lacquer, red brick, fern;
An open briefcase, scattered memos, the night;
Cell phone silent, bit lip, a pause that burned and burned.

4

The Late Qing

1

One leaf, torn from my saddle-stitched
Journal, floats in the emperor's
Most strangled lane of golden stone
And in the deadest-end *hutong*
Rife with the slap of cards and steamed
Winter dumplings of doomed Beijing.
You will script my partitioned memory.
Cranes, in error, cantilever sky.
The cement heavens; the dates awry.

2

Even my head upon your shoulder
Was subject to imperial surveillance
And to our own knowledge of circumstance
Lifting my flushed ear from your collar
Bone. Our longing, watched from all angles,
Summed up the Age of Frustration.
I watch you move in crowded rooms.
Lift your chopsticks slowly to my lips.
Look at what they whisper to themselves.

3

Afterwards, he dreamed that when she slept
Not touching him, her mind afloat
Became the mind of the entire billion,
Her remote body *zhongxin* of *zhongguo*
From cattle-dark slopes above Ulaanbataar
To thin cries beneath hammering streets
Where cities of orphans dozed in wait
For the crowing wrench of dawn, dreaming
Of a man untouched in his sleep.

4

The teetering life. The lifelong clench.
The pure arch, broken: a cramping bow.
If the inward curve is incomplete,
A thin wooden block where nails meet.
Stilt that adds nothing to your height.
Dear mother teaches you, daily,
Unwrapping of the golden lilies.
Mistress lets you lean against a wall.
In the end, you are wondrously small.

5

Not her loveliness that lashed me down
But her thirst and shining desperation.
I sought her at the swollen river border
Between the Yellow Warlord and the Red,
Cattle dead, the village scholars starved.
A single truss of broken bridge remained.
My children gripped the tightrope where it frayed,
The currents choked with cholera and hope.
To reach her side, I tore their hands away.

6

The heat rises; the petals fall.
Old men emerge in the evenings
With a plainly crafted bamboo cage
Pendulant from each hand, balancing
Their shuffling gate. Blue cloth slippers.
On low stools they soothe their crooked knees
In little sidewalk clans, feed their sparrows
With an exquisite pathos
They learned in the revolution.

7

"I remember." "Your memory must fill
With forgetting." "I am better at wanting."
"You must be better at wanting to forget."
Words stretched, a wire of sound
Over the raw scream. "One cannot seek want."
"Remove the thoughts, but love me still."
"On what level?" "The reach, without touch."
Each shining terrace, thinnest of film.
Early spring, green rice in water.

8

The air was close, awaiting thunder.
All day we drifted on green water,
Circled like the shadow of the carp
That circled like our own good fortune
In the other world. The riverbanks burned.
Small boys were selling name brand water.
On an island in the midst made love
At last, fled home over shadowless glass,
The realm surrounding us a flaming wall.

9

When she wept. Paint only the stems.
When she laughed. Mark the sundial's tip.
When her breast flowed. Strophes of adverbs.
When she licked, lingering, your chest . . .
When she howled. From exiled Kunming
Fill silken scrolls with a single tone.
When she turned away. Trace the new moon.
When she smiled through tears. Lay petals.
When she wept. Paint only the stems.

5

The Shadow Photon

The Shadow Photon

One need only look a little more closely to see the first
clue of parallel universes. . . . Something is still deflect-
ing that solitary photon from its path. . . . Further
experiments with mirrors and lenses show that the
entities that are doing the interfering behave exactly like
photons—except that they are invisible.
                                        —David Deutsch

Ghost light. Day after day the rains of Carolina
Poured into the winter forests of Quebec.

The isotherms knotted in a third dimension,
Warm air shelving over arctic like the junctions

Of tectonic plates—these relentless iterations
Of his thoughts through different zones of glass,

Oriental fans and the last, systaltic days:
With her dying, the painted pattern folds away

Into a single depth, the sequence disappears,
The years make, after all,

                              a simple silhouette.

His greenhouse in the garden is a lens of warmth
Riding up each morning on the deep of storm,

While he putters, while she sleeps.

In doorways now he often shivers at a light
With no true shadows, a light that bends and frays.

In those first hours the freezing, steady rain
Was tame, a moistening of cold-dried trees.

On evening walks along the river, toward her bed,
He watched the twigs grow slick, a rich and lissome black,

Each raindrop as a photon counteracting night,
Slow laying out of patterned light from some remote

Extreme. He moved beneath a thousand crooked seams
Of luminosity—the gleam, toward dawn,

A deeper oil as the rain held.

The second day, a heavier shellac,
A thicker lamination of the sweet south mist;

The third, translucent manacles on every branch,
Dark cortex cinched and blanched in milky shells,

The snow's crust pebbled like the office door
He once passed through to volunteer for war.

He was afraid the inside-outedness was now complete,
Mere scarf and numbing feet and fumbling mortal lips,

The core of what went on.

On the fourth day, the shapely maples hunching down—
Further rains of hard light still to come.

—·—

Months afterward the most disfigured trees
Surprised him with prolific crops of seed.

Awkward, elbowed—the remaining boughs of maples
Went green, then brown with bristled clumps of keys,

Each local breeze releasing into sundogged air
A hurried flight of flashing scimitars,

Single-bladed dervishes to thickly stud the lawn
And clog the troughs and drainpipes out of season.

—·—

Throughout, his bleb eye glued
To the light-bleeding slit

In the perfected wall
Of their experiment

(He has seen this pressure—
Membranous surge and thrum—

Where the lees-of-burgundy red
Of a sumac's seed cone tip

Vibrates without motion
Against the snow-white snow),

A micrometer slit
In the heliotropic

Slit, but anyway insists
Everyday experience

Teaches that light travels
Simply, in straight lines,

(Even how effortless
To forget it moves

At all, is not already
There), and therefore casts

Shadows that are silhouettes
Abstracted from the forms

Of obstacles in its path,
Tension of the grey laths

Of evening on his forehead
Where his fixed fear watched—

The burgundy lees
Against her cotton shift.

But the laboratory
Of enduring study

The magnification
Of shadow's clean edge

Shows the hedging of zones,
Whispers: what if shadow

Draws no line with light?
The year the scientists write

A closely measured look
Unhooks the first latch

Of parallel realms, reveals
That light tends to bend and fray

At the border of shade.
She breathes. His bleb eye maps.

———

The last greenhouse he framed in their narrow yard
Was carpentered for north, shed shards of ice from its steep pitch
At a glove's tap, shrugging them clear like surplus panes.
Daily the rain. The snow grew littered with translucent skiffs.

I was brief time itself. From the back lane gate
Each weak winter dawn I could just make out his shape

Moving in that glowing box—

Wooden sash and glass: the door and walls and A-frame roof
All old storm windows waterproofed with tin, re-angled.
A jerry rig of tangled cords brought power from the house
To run a baseboard heater and fluorescent bulbs;

Cribbed two-by-fours and plywood; sawhorse; pink clay pots;
Rich whiffs of rot and roots from tubs of muck
Scavenged from the bog bed where the river feeds the lake.
And never silent. Ice rain on the glass like tacks.

Just room for two to stand and talk—

This was the week he noticed that her eyes were dull
As though all light that touched them now was sinking in.
She didn't know him. Time permitting I would stop to chat.
In the middle of a sentence he would notice me again

And stare in awe as if I had become
A vision of beauty—which, all local eyes perceive,
I'm not. His glasses fogged. But quickly he would find
His senses, see me as I was, and be old
And overkind again, and still. Each time this happened

I pointed through the feeble light to fresh-turned soil,
His winter toil, and asked what he had planted.
It wouldn't be peas, he'd say, I know it wouldn't be peas.
He had the feeling he had answered me. I slipped away.

—·—

After the hours at her bedside, after his thumb
Draws a thousand slow circles on the back of her hand,

The sea would revisit his dreaming after so many years,
Horizon a dark canting mirror—

The universe of water unseen and surrounding—
Like the war, like the ocean's Jute and Saxon serpents

Hunting the convoys. Words came out of the night
As a tightening pulse, his fingers fluttered replies,

His thumb ached—

A Caribbean breath into the mouth of winter;
The rains rained until the splintering began

There, in his waiting; tracing the fan-vaulting
In cathedrals of glass. A slight fault. A rifle crack

Through the albescent woods, through the black-less-ness
Of the negative: bone bright and hot, all flesh

As shadows in the background of the film.
A maiming split, accelerating coal chute rush,

A slow motion chandelier of ice swung free,
A veined fragility unstrung.

He tries to divine the next shifting of sea
Awake in the bushland thickets by the river

Where the invisible droplets
Are particles disturbing their phantoms of light,

Silent in air but touching the world
With small clicks; like words; making his fingertips itch

And sense the blood of signals through the arm
And a ship's alarms on the North Atlantic run

Astride green ghost-soundings of the radar,
The storm a wild Morse he will never quite transcribe.

—·—

Look grandpa, said the grandson,
At all those pretty trees. They've
Learned to catch and hold the rain.

Coda

The Smallness Between the Stars

Somewhere the red reveals conclusively orange,
And the sense of spectrum begins—
Blood orange between your lips.

Some particular flake through slow winter morning
Is just enough—at lunch I look
And brown fields are cold white ash.

"Somewhere," he wrote, in a nightfall whisper of grief,
"The sea deepens from blue to black"
(And somewhere from crystal to blue).

The thinning hold of exosphere somewhere dissolves
A last molecule of breath
And a song without words begins.

The voice abandoned on the darkening porch
Calls out to a certain distance
And then can reach no further.

There is a place, and an instant, on a torn match
Where the faint yellow lesion buds
From bituminous soil.

There is the moment before, and the moment after
The coming of each salt thought of you
Out of somewhere, and into sometime;

But the unthinkable map of their emerging
    Is everywhere we can never be.
    And with this our love contends.

Notes to the poems

p. *21* "the field dancing out of the braking cosmic vacuum."
Timothy Ferris, *The Whole Shebang: A State-of-the-Universe Report,* p. 241.

p. *53* "hutong." The small alleyways of Beijing's old neigh-
bourhoods, now fast disappearing.

p. *55* "zhongxin." Heart, the centre of the centre.
"zhongguo." The Middle Kingdom.

p. *75* "Somewhere the sea deepens from blue to black."
Philip Levine, *The Mercy.*

About the Author

David Manicom's most recent book *is Progeny of Ghosts: Travels in Russia and the Old Empire*, an account of his three years living in the former Soviet Union. It was the winner of the Quebec Writer's Federation 1998 Mavis Gallant Award for non-fiction, and was short-listed for the Writer's Development Trust Viacom Award for Non-fiction. *The Montreal Gazette* called it an "exquisite book." He is the author of three acclaimed collections of poetry. *Books In Canada* has called him a writer "to read, quote, study and memorize," and the *Halifax Chronicle-Herald* wrote that "[he] is the most skilled writer of English poetry in Canada today." His first collection of stories, *Ice In Dark Water* (1997), won the Mordecai Richler's Prix Parizeau, and was short-listed for the Danuta Gleed award. The Globe and Mail wrote: "he is a talented and challenging writer who deserves a significant and enlightened audience." David Manicom grew up in rural Ontario and has lived in Toronto, Montreal, Moscow and Islamabad. He has recently returned to Canada from his posting in Beijing.